GERMAN EXISTENTIALISM

MARTIN HEIDEGGER

GERMAN EXISTENTIALISM

Translated from the German, and with an Introduction by

DAGOBERT D. RUNES

The Wisdom Library
a division of
Philosophical Library
New York

15 East 40 Street, New York 16, N. Y.

Library of Congress Catalog Card No. 65-18053

The publishers wish to give due credit to Guido Schneeberger's magnificent compilation, *Nachlese zu Heidegger*: *Dokumente zu seinem Leben und Denken.*

ISBN 978-0-80653079-6

Distributed to the Trade
by BOOK SALES, INC.
New York

Printed in the United States of America

There is a yellowish grey wolf, who, winters, joins the pack, roaming the icy tundras of Siberia, sparing neither man, animal, nor child. In the heat of the summer, however, when the brush is dry and lifeless, he crawls into the peasant's back yard, licking his hands, whining for food. Such is the nature of man and the brevity of memory that the peasant feeds the bloody tooth of this rapacious beast.

— Count Leo Tolstoy

CONTENTS

INTRODUCTION

I am presenting this small collection of speeches, statements and appeals by Martin Heidegger with a considerable amount of uneasiness. These documents — and they are only a few from the vast evidence available — are bound to throw the light of simple reasoning and simple ethical awareness upon a widely known philosopher who, by joining the National Socialist Party of Adolf Hitler, brought discredit not only upon his distinguished teacher, Edmund Husserl, but also upon the philosophical profession.

Heidegger himself once defined philosophy as the search for the meaning of being. We heard him as a young man proclaiming the Nietzschean insight that God is death, that man lives engulfed by nothingness, and that man in all his complicated mentality is forever becoming, never really being.

Martin Heidegger avoided whenever possible the use of accepted metaphysical terminology, engaging himself in the process of intricate word coinage which made it quite difficult for the non-initiated to find their way through his labyrinthine *Weltanschauung.*

But I am not at the moment interested in interpreting the existentialist philosophy or theology of this follower of Soren Kierkegaard who turned into a follower of Adolf Hitler.

I must say initially that, in my eyes, word coins that are used interchangeably for metaphysics and for National Socialism are counterfeit. It is a cheerless task for me to prove by the translation and presentation of Heidegger's own words that he has betrayed by doing so German philosophy in particular and philosophy in general.

From the days of the early Vedas of India, the Tao Te King of China, the early wisdom literature of the Hebrews and the meditations of Heraclitus, Socrates, Plato and Aristotle, to the very presence of contemporary thinkers like Whitehead, Santayana, Einstein and Bergson, marking such giants in between as Bacon, Descartes, Spinoza, Locke, Kant — all through these thousands of years philosophy was there, the queen of the sciences.

The world stood still in the face of philosophy, because she served neither time, secular ambitions, nor purposeful deflections. Philosophy was the search for the perennial good and the understanding of the perennial ideas.

Then there came a man from the ranks of the professional philosophers — those dedicated to the search for the highest good — who made the queen a handmaiden of a villainous; monstrous demagogue.

Martin Heidegger joined the sinister cabal of Hitler, Himmler, Goering and Streicher, the church busters, the art defilers, the perverters of history, the defamers of jurisprudence, and the grand assassins of millions of women, children, and aged.

And how masterfully Martin Heidegger managed to weave into the sanguinary pattern of National Socialism the pseudo-profundity of his metaphysical terminology!

Here are some prize quotations from the pen of Heidegger, the neo-existentialist:

> "The National Socialist Revolution is not simply the taking of power in the state by one party from another, but brings a complete revolution of our German existence." "The Führer himself, and only he, is the current and future reality of Germany, and his word is your law." "We have completely broken with the idolization of a landless and powerless thinking. We see the end of all philosophy which could serve it. We are certain of this: that clear toughness and security about the plain questions of the nature of being are returning to us."
>
> "Now there is a sharp battle to be fought in the spirit of National Socialism, which must not stifle on account of humanistic, Christian notions that hold us down by their imprecision. It is also not sufficient to pay lip service to the New Order, since one paints everything with a certain political color. Of the greatest danger to us are the noncommittal plans and slogans that are everywhere springing up, but that lead only to self-deception, just like the 'new' concept of science, which is nothing more than the old, dressed up with a few anthropological trimmings."

Perhaps there were others in the history of philosophy whose escutcheons were tinted with the splatter of personal deviation or lack of integrity as inherent in their status; but never has one yet come forth among the cogitators of the past to drop so low as to make his whole involved metaphysical structure the underpinnings of a vicious, despotic scheme.

I do not doubt that scientists and technicians, artisans and craftsmen, can be accomplished in their respective fields of endeavor and yet serve an evil master. But the philosopher is not a scientist, he is not a craftsman, he is not a technician, and his only contribution to the wide community is his love of wisdom and his wisdom of love. And if such have deserted him he becomes another robot of the infernal crew of tyranny, and all his involved verbiage is just an evil breath in the wind of time.

D. D. R.

THE PHILOSOPHER HEIDEGGER ENTERS THE NAZI PARTY*

A German Editorial

On the day of German Labor, on the day of the Community of the People, the Rector of Freiburg University, Dr. Martin Heidegger, made his official entry into the National Socialist Party. We Freiburg Nazis see in this act more than a superficial acknowledgment of the revolution that has been accomplished and of the powers that be. We know that Martin Heidegger, in his high sense of responsibility, in his concern for the destiny and future of the German people, stands in the midst of our glorious movement. We know, too, that he has never made any secret of his German character, that *for years he has supported the party of Adolf Hitler* in its difficult struggle for existence and power to the utmost of his strength, that he was always ready to bring a sacrifice to Germany's holy altar, and that no National Socialist ever knocked in vain at his door.

We Freiburg people are proud that this profound thinker works at our University, and that he has, in

* *Der Alemanne,* May 3, 1933.

refusing an honorable call, made it clear that he wishes to remain bound to our beautiful home town, which is also his. As National Socialists we find endless satisfaction in the knowledge that this great man stands in our ranks, in Adolf Hitler's ranks. Like our Leader, the philosopher Martin Heidegger sprang, by will power and strength of spirit, from the restricted circles of an insignificant country town to a shining position in the learned world. We shall not be far wrong if we attribute to that origin, to the unconcealed loyalty to his country home, that very strength which enables modern philosophy, in the person of Heidegger, to go beyond the blind spot and lead on to fruitful problems. Starting from the phenomenology of Edmund Husserl, Heidegger has, by the radical nature of his approach, created a completely new situation in modern philosophy. His chief work, *Existence and Time,* involves a crisis, a turning point, which in its significance and scope can be compared only to the impact of Kantian philosophy upon Occidental thought.

Just as Kant conquered the petrified dichotomy of empiricism and rationalism, because instead of attempting an unfruitful synthesis he pressed on beyond and behind the opposing philosophical positions to the origin, to the original unity behind the dichotomy, so, too, Heidegger by his profundity has drawn the teeth of the modern dichotomy between idealism and realism that has degenerated into a lifeless formalism very far from its origins. He has thereby demonstrated that a theory can never be finished off by critical comparisons, but only by creative thought, whose originator, seen from the point of the too overwhelming contrast, seems by himself and without further aid to be ineffectual. It is a characteristic of our spiritual life that we turn away from the flatness of positivism and naturalism, which present no problems, and turn to the problems of metaphysics that soar even beyond the limits of Kantian criticism.

But whereas this turning toward metaphysics appears in other contemporary thinkers predominantly as a reaction that is a link with pre-Kantian traditions without being ready for Kantianism, in Martin Heidegger it has been creatively realized. His philosophy is far from playing off Aristotle against Kant; insofar as it opens up the old ontology, it can reveal the metaphysical motives of Kantian philosophy and enable the great German thinker to grasp the hidden origins of his philosophizing, not only from outdated theories, but from the living sources.

The effect of Heidegger's philosophy is powerful today. Every serious researcher must, whether he rejects it or agrees with it, start from the assumption that it represents the core of modern philosophical thought, and that its creator, Martin Heidegger, is the spiritual leader of contemporary thinking. We are proud of Martin Heidegger; we greet him with all honor. As once Fichte did not deny his spiritual power and authority over the uprising of 1813, so Heidegger has recognized and fulfilled the greatness of our era.

INAUGURATION OF NEW RECTOR*

A German News Report

The Alma Mater of Freiburg had its great day today. In the presence of the Minister for Culture, Education and Justice Dr. Wacker, Minister of the Interior Pflaumer, the rectors of the Heidelberg and Karlsruhe colleges, the Mayor, Dr. Kerber, and many guests of honor, the rectorate was formally transferred to the new Rector, Professor of Philosophy Dr. Martin Heidegger.

For the first time the storm troops of Adolf Hitler could appear freely, and the brown ceremonial uniform gave new luster to the impressive scene. The orchestra, directed by Professor Gurlitt, played Brahms' "Academic Festival Overture," which owes its origin to the honorary degree bestowed on the master by the University of Breslau in 1881. The thematic content combines original melodies with the melodies of well-known songs of both serious and lighthearted character, and concludes with the joyous "Gaudeamus Igitur."

The outgoing Rector, Dr. Sauer, gave an overview

* *Der Alemanne*, May 28, 1933, page 11.

of the previous semester, which marked the end of a period of superficiality and spiritual pauperization, and the beginning of a movement from which there can be no turning back.

Professor Heidegger made a very important speech on "The Self-Assertion of the German Universities."

THE SELF-ASSERTION OF THE GERMAN UNIVERSITIES*

A Lecture by Prof. Heidegger

Acceptance of the Rectorate entails an obligation to become the spiritual leader of this noble college. The loyalty of the teaching and student bodies awakes and becomes stronger only if there is a true and common rootedness in the tradition of the German universities. This tradition, however, only attains clarity, prestige and power, when the leaders themselves are guided by the inexorability of that spiritual order that stamps the destiny of the German people with the imprint of its history. It produces true coinage only if we accept the tradition from the very foundations upwards. Some people see the traditionally administrative character of the university in its self-government. Self-government will remain with us, but it is founded upon self-recollection, and exists only in the strength of the self-assertion of the German Universities. This is on the one hand adherence to tradition, on the other hand a drive toward knowledge as a drive toward the historical-spiritual order of the German people.

* *Freiburger Zeitung,* May 29, 1933, page 6.

Knowledge and German destiny must come to power above all in the adherence to tradition, and will do so only when teachers and students alike suspend knowledge as their innermost need, and participate in the destiny of Germany in its most extreme need. If the teachers of the university take their places in the posts of greatest danger in the current world state of uncertainty, they will become masters of leadership. The decisive quality of a leader is his power to continue alone, not out of pride and lust for power, but out of a sense of duty. Strength of this kind confirms that a man has been rightly selected, and wins for him a true following. The German student body is ready and resolved to stand by Germany in her hour of need. And therein adherence to the tradition of the university finds its expression; it is a true expression insofar as the student body, through the new student law, places itself under the law of its tradition. To give oneself a code of laws is itself the highest form of freedom. The much-sung academic freedom will vanish; it was false because it was only negative, implying uncommittedness in thought and act. The concept of the freedom of the German student will be brought back to reality.

In the future will flourish the threefold commitment and service of the German student body, once in the community of the people through the Labor Service; again to the honor of the nation through Army Service; and a third time in commitment to the spiritual order of the German people through the service of learning. These three binding ties are fundamental to the German tradition; they are equally necessary and of equal value.

The German Universities will only attain power if the three forms of service unite in overwhelming force, if both teachers and students in their adherence to tradition place themselves side by side in the thick of the fight. All the powers of the heart and all the skills of the body are developed through struggle, are strengthened in battle, and are proven by continuing the fight. *We first understand the glory and the greatness of the Hitler revolution* when we carry implanted deep within us this reflection: Everything that is great is in the midst of the storm.

LABOR SERVICE AND THE UNIVERSITY*

In the future the schools will no longer hold an exclusive position in the realm of education. A new and decisive educational force has arisen in the form of the Labor Service. The Hitler Labor Camp is contiguous with the old people's home, the youth club, the army barracks and the school.

In the Labor Camp the State has realized a new and immediate revelation of the community of the people. Henceforth every young German will be ruled by knowledge about labor, in which is gathered the strength of the people, so that he may therein experience the hardness of his existence, feel the driving power of his own will, and appreciate anew the diversity of his capabilities. The Hitler Labor Camp is at the same time a valuable training ground for leadership in all walks and callings of life, for there participation and cooperation count above all things, while passivity and looking on count for nothing.

The Hitler Labor Camp awakes and develops knowl-

* *Freiburger Studentenzeitung,* June 20, 1933, page 1.

edge of the working community in all walks of life, and this same knowledge, deeply rooted in the young German, will henceforth be a purifying and order-bringing influence upon what the school can and cannot do, upon what it should and should not be.

The Hitler Labor Camp, as a unique educational environment, will become a new source of those strengths through which all other educational powers — above all the schools — will be compelled to a decision and thereby changed.

Our college is surrounded in the near neighborhood by Labor Camps staffed by teachers of this college. A new reality exists in the Labor Camp. It stands as a symbol, signifying that our noble school is open to the new educational power of Labor Service. Camp and college are disposed, in mutual give and take, to co-operate in bringing the educational forces of the people into a new and deeply rooted unity out of which the people pledge to their State activity and participation in the destiny of the country.

Heil Hitler
HEIDEGGER

THE UNIVERSITY UNDER THE NEW REICH*

An address by Professor Martin Heidegger to the students of Heidelberg University

After a greeting from the president of the Heidelberg student body, Professor Heidegger said, among other things:

We have on the one hand the new Reich, and on the other the university, that must take its tasks from the Reich's will to survive. There is a revolution in Germany, and we must ask ourselves, "Is there a revolution in the university?" No. The fighting is still in the skirmishing stage, and has so far mounted only a single attack — the building of a new life in the Hitler Labor Camps — and in the educational circles close to our college has taken from us those educational tasks to which we hitherto thought we had sole claim.

There is always the possibility that the university may sink into oblivion and kiss good-bye any educa-

* *Heidelberger Neueste Nachrichten,* July 1, 1933, page 4.

tional power. But it must be incorporated anew into the community of the people and bind itself to the State. The university must become once more a force in education, that may impel the leaders of our State from knowledge to new knowledge. The goal is threefold: (1) knowledge of the contemporary university; (2) knowledge of the current dangers that threaten our future; and (3) a new courage.

Hitherto the university has researched and taught in the same way for many decades. Research was supposed to lead to teaching, and a comfortable compromise between the two was sought. It was out of this attitude that the viewpoint of the teachers was formed — nobody ever worried about the state of the university as a community. The sea of research was shoreless, and hid its uncertainties behind the idea of the international advance of learning; teaching became goalless, and hid itself behind a tangle of examination regulations.

Now there is a sharp battle to be fought in the spirit of National Socialism, which must not stifle on account of humanistic, Christian notions that hold us down by their imprecision. It is also not sufficient to pay lip service to the New Order, since one paints everything with a certain political color. Of the greatest danger to us are the noncommittal plans and slogans that are everywhere springing up, but that lead only to self-deception, just like the "new" concept of science, which is nothing more than the old, dressed up with a few anthropological trimmings. And all this talk of "politics" is a nuisance, because old humdrum habits will not be given a new drive by it. The only serious token of identification with the New Order is the experience of need, the aggressive grappling with reality.

Only those actions are justified that follow the lead of an inner pledge to the future. The cry has already gone up "Learning is in danger because of today's crazy devotion to military sports . . . and so forth." But what's the good of wasting time here, when it's a question of fighting for the State! Danger never came of working for the State, but only from indifference and resistance. Therefore only true strength, not halfheartedness, holds the possibility of following the right road.

The new courage clearly reveals all these dangers. It alone opens one's eyes to what is coming and developing. It compels every teacher and every student to make a decision on the basic questions of learning, and this decision is final, for upon it depends whether we Germans will remain a learned people, in the highest sense of the word. The new teaching is not a matter of making useful contacts, but of freedom to learn and to make a contribution to learning.

It means allowing oneself to be oppressed by the unknown, and then making oneself master over it in clear understanding, and becoming secure in one's perception of reality. It is out of such teaching that true research awakes. It is bound up with the whole because it is rooted in the people and bound to the State. The student will be swung out into the uncertainty of all things, and will learn the necessity of taking risks. Study must once again become a gamble, with no protection for the cowardly. Whoever does not survive the fight will be left to lie on the field of battle. The new courage must become accustomed to constancy, for according to the leaders, the battle will go on for a long time. *It will be fought with all the strength of the new Reich, which Chancellor Hitler will bring to reality.* It must be fought by a hard race of men who take no thought for themselves, and who live constantly under ordeal, ever striving toward their goal. The fight concerns the image of the university teacher and leader!

GERMAN STUDENTS*

The National Socialist Revolution brings a complete revolution in our German existence.

In these circumstances, it is up to you to remain tough and full of drive, developing yourselves and ready for anything.

Your will to knowledge seeks to experience what is essential, what is simple, what is great. It is demanded of you that you become those who drive furthest and are most deeply pledged.

Be hard and righteous in your demands.

Remain clear and secure in your rejection of the false.

The knowledge that you struggle for does not lead to conceited self-possession. It appears as the primary quality of the leader who answers the call of the State. You can no longer be only listeners. You are pledged to know and to act, cooperating in the shaping of the new school of the German spirit. Each one of you must now prove your talents and abilities and use them in the right place. That happens through the power of

* *Freiburger Studentenzeitung,* November 3, 1933, page 1.

aggressive action within the ring of the whole people that surrounds you.

May your loyalty and willingness to follow grow stronger every day and every hour! May your courage to make sacrifices grow greater continuously, for the survival and increase of the power of our people.

Doctrine and "ideas" shall no longer govern your existence. The *Führer* himself, and only he, is the current and future reality of Germany, and his word is your law. Learn to know ever more deeply within you: "From now on every matter demands determination and every action demands responsibility."

Heil Hitler!
MARTIN HEIDEGGER

AVOWAL TO ADOLF HITLER AND THE NATIONAL STATE*

Heidegger's address at the election meeting of German Scholars in Leipzig on November 11, 1933

German Teachers and Comrades! German compatriots!

The German people is called by the *Führer* to a choice; but the *Führer* begs nothing of the people, but rather gives them the freest choice whether the entire people desires its own survival or not. Tomorrow the people will choose nothing less than what its future is to be.

This choice cannot be compared to previous choices. Its unique quality is simply the greatness of the decision to be taken. The inexorability of the simple and of the ultimate allows no hesitation and no delay. This final decision reaches out to the uttermost boundaries of our

* Pledge of the professors of German universities and colleges to Adolf Hitler and the National Socialist State. Published by the National Socialist Teachers' Association (*Nazionalsozialistische Lehrerbund*) Dresden, 1933, page 13ff.

people. And what are these boundaries? They consist in that primordial demand of every being that he find his own way to salvation. But there is a great separation between what can and cannot be expected of a people. By the power of this principle the German people preserves the worthiness and individuality of its existence. The will to be responsible to itself alone is not only the fundamental principle of our people, but also the fundamental consequence of the effect of its National Socialist State. Out of this determination to be responsible to itself comes every work of every class. The work of the classes carries and strengthens the living structure of the State. It gives back to the people their roots in the land; it places the State in the position of being the realization of the people in the field of influence of all existing powers of human existence.

It was not lust for honor, nor a seeking after fame, nor blind obstinacy nor power-seeking that demanded of the *Führer* our resignation from the League of Nations, but simply the clear determination to be unconditionally responsible to ourselves in enduring and mastering our own destiny. That resignation is not a withdrawal from other peoples. On the contrary, by that step our people placed itself under the law of survival, to which every people must owe allegiance if it is to remain a people. It is precisely out of that common response to the unconditional demand for responsibility to self that first arises the possibility of mutual respect, and thereby of assent to a true community. The determination to have a true community of the peoples is as far from being an unstable, noncommital world brotherhood as it is from being a blind rule of power. The determination works beyond that contrast; it fosters an open and manly independence and cooperation of peoples and States.

What happens in such a case? Is there a return to barbarism? No! It is a turning away from every empty action and hidden intrigue through the demands of responsibility for one's own action. Is there an outbreak of lawlessness? No! It is a clear avowal of the inviolable individuality of every people. Is there a renunciation of the creativity of a spiritual people and the destruction of its historical traditions? No! It is the breakthrough of a purified youth drawing strength from its own roots. Its adherence to the State will make this people hard on itself and respectful toward every genuine undertaking.

What kind of event is this, then? The people is winning back the truth of its will to survive, for truth is the revelation of whatever a people makes secure, clear and strong in its actions and knowledge. From such truth springs the real desire to know. And this desire to know determines the claims of knowledge. And from there the boundaries are finally determined within which questioning and research are founded and must prove themselves. It is from such origins that scholarship is founded. It is bound up with the necessity of autonomous national existence. Whence it comes that scholarship is the educational passion, tamed by this necessity, for wanting to know in order to act wisely. To be wise means for us to be mighty in making things clear and to be resolved upon action.

We have completely broken with the idolization of

a landless and powerless thinking. We see the end of all philosophy which could serve it. We are certain of this: that clear toughness and security about the plain question of the nature of being are returning to us. The courage to cut loose from what exists, and either to grow or to break, is the innermost motivation behind the question of popular scholarship. For courage looks forward, frees itself from the past, dares the unaccustomed and the unforeseeable. For us it is not a question of the uncommitted play of curiosity, nor is it the obstinate clinging to skepticism at all costs. Questioning means to us to place ourselves outside the idea of the prime importance of objects and their laws; it means not shutting ourselves up in the terror of the untamed and the chaos of darkness. For the sake of this questioning we will certainly continue to question, and will not remain in the service of those who have grown old and tired and who seek comfortable answers. We know that questioning courage to experience and to endure the abyss of existence is already a higher form of answer than any cheap information given by artificially constructed systems of thought.

And so we avow to those who will shortly be entrusted with the protection of our people's desire to know: The National Socialist Revolution is not simply the taking of power in the state by one party from another, but brings a complete revolution of our German existence. Henceforth every matter demands decision, and every act demands responsibility.

Of this we are certain: If the will to autonomous responsibility becomes the foundation of the community of peoples, then every people can and must teach every other people about its riches and about the power of all great deeds and undertakings in human existence.

The choice that the German people must now make is, merely as an event and without reference to the decision, the strongest avowal of the new German reality of the National Socialist State. Our resolve to be responsible to ourselves alone demands that each people seek and guard the greatness and truth of its own choice. This resolve is the highest citadel of peace between peoples, for it binds itself to manly watchfulness and absolute honor. *The Führer has awakened this resolve in the whole people and has fused it into a single resolution.* No man can remain aloof on the day of the manifestation of this resolve!

Heil Hitler!

HEIDEGGER

THE CALL TO LABOR SERVICE

*A Lecture by Professor Heidegger**

The new road to the education of our German youth leads through Hitler Labor Service.

This service provides a deep experience of toughness, down-to-earthness, of the strength and legitimacy of the simplest and most realistic work within the framework of the group.

This service provides a deep experience of the clarity and confirmation of the continuity of tradition that is subject to daily trial and decision, and experience of the responsibility of the individual toward the people to which he belongs.

This service provides a deep experience of the foundations of true comradeship, which develops only through the pressure of a great common danger, or through continually growing devotion to a task whose results can be grasped; it has nothing to do with the sentimental exchange of emotional outpourings between in-

* *Freiburger Studentenzeitung*, January 23, 1934, page 1.

dividuals who have agreed to eat, sleep and sing under the same roof.

This service provides a deep experience of the effective condition for a true consciousness of individuality, and takes the final decision concerning a choice of profession out of the realm of bourgeois and expedient reckoning of prospects.

We must consider the effect, already visible, of the Labor Service upon current life, and learn to grasp that it is preparing a mighty enrichment of the German existence of our growing youth. In the German colleges a new foundation for scholarly work will slowly emerge. On this account the concept of "spirit" and "spiritual work" that has hitherto flourished among the educated, and which its supporters wish even now to save because of a unique quality of spiritual creativeness, will vanish utterly. Only then shall we learn that work is spiritual in its own right. The animal and the almost animal cannot work, for they lack the fundamental experience required — that of decisive action toward a task, the ability to stand firm in resolution once an order has been received — in short they lack freedom, that is to say, spirit. A so-called "spiritual undertaking" justifies that name, not because it is directed toward "higher spiritual matters," but only when as an undertaking it reaches far back into the need of the *historical existence* of a people, and is effectively — because consciously — motivated by the toughness and danger of human existence.

There exists only one single German "way of life." It is that which is rooted in the enduring core of the people and in a way of work freely offered to the will of the State, *a way whose enrichment is being shaped in the National Socialist Revolution.* The lame, the complacent, the halfhearted will go into the Hitler Labor Service because to remain aloof would perhaps endanger their examination results or prospects of obtaining an appointment. The strong and unbroken, who permeate their existence with the secret of a new future for our people, are proud that toughness is demanded of them; for this is the moment when they approach the hardest tasks, that bring neither reward nor praise, but only joy in readiness for sacrifice and service in the realm of the innermost necessities of German existence.

FOLLOW THE FUHRER*

On October 30, 1933 the Mayor's employment program found work for 600 unemployed. The auxiliary services of child care and clothing sensibly bettered the conditions of the workers, so that now their National Socialist education can begin. On the 22nd of this month (February, 1934) the 600 marched to the largest lecture hall of the university and were greeted by the Rector in the following address:

German compatriots! German workers! As Rector of the university I greet you most heartily in this house. This greeting marks the beginning of our work together. We will begin by making clear the meaning of the till now unheard-of event, that you, relief workers of the town of Freiburg, have met us in the largest lecture hall of the university. What does this event mean?

Through widespread and entirely new methods of work procurement, the town of Freiburg has led you to employment and food. And because of that you are

* *Der Alemanne,* February 1, 1934, evening edition, page 9.

favored over the other unemployed men of the town. But this privilege has its duties, too.

And your duty is to take the employment, and perform the tasks, in whatever manner the *Führer* of our new State demands. For employment is not merely the lifting of extreme poverty, it is not merely the putting aside of inner hopelessness or despair, nor merely protection from harassment; it is equally and uniquely a building up in the new future of our people.

The employment procurement service must make workers and unemployed comrades alike active in and for the State, and thereby in and for the whole people. The compatriot who gets work will find that he is not cast off and left to fend for himself, but that he belongs to the people, and that every service and every achievement has its own value and leads on to other tasks and achievements. From this experience he will win back his self-respect and a proud bearing, and will be able to show firmness and decision in meeting his comrades.

The goal is to work hard for a satisfying existence as a member of the German community of peoples.

But to do this you must know where you stand as a member of this people; you must know how the people incorporates its members and by this incorporation renews itself; you must know what is happening to the people in this National Socialist State; you must know what a hard struggle it will be to bring this new reality to fruition; you must know what the coming healing of the body of the German people means, and what it demands from each individual; you must know to what a pretty pass German men have come because of urbanization, and how they will be given back to the soil and the land through settlements, *you must know the implications of the fact that eighteen million Germans belong to the German people, but not to the German State because they live beyond the state frontiers.*

Every working man of our people must know for what reason and to what end he stands there. Through this living, and always current, knowledge will his life first be rooted in the whole German people and in its destiny. And with the procurement of employment goes the procurement of this knowledge, and it is your right, and indeed your duty, to demand this knowledge and to make every effort to come by it.

And now your young comrades of the university stand ready to help you get the knowledge. They are resolved to help, so that the knowledge may unfold in you and grow, and never again sleep. They will help you, not as "scholars," from the "upper" classes, but as comrades of the people who have recognized your duty.

They will not come to you as "educated" people condescending to a class, or even a "lower class," of uneducated men, but as comrades. They will listen to your questions, your needs, your difficulties and your doubts, talk these through with you, and by your common work bring you to clarity, freedom and decision. And so, what does it mean that we are met here in this hall of the university?

It is a sign that there exists a new common resolve to throw up a bridge between those who labor with their hands and those who perform brain work. This resolve is no longer an empty dream — and why not? *Because through the National Socialist State our entire German reality has been altered, and that means altering all our previous ideas and thinking, too.*

The words "knowledge" and "scholarship" have acquired a different meaning, and so too have the words "work" and "worker."

Scholarship is not the possession of a restricted class of citizens to misuse as a weapon for the exploitation of those who do the work; it is only a stronger and therefore more responsible form of that knowledge that the whole German people must demand and seek for the sake of its historico-political existence, if this people desires to safeguard its continuation and greatness. The knowledge of true scholarship does not differ in its tradition from the knowledge of farmers, lumberjacks, miners and craftsmen. For knowledge means being at home in the world in which we live as individuals and as part of a community.

Knowledge means growth of resolve and action in the performance of a task that has been given us, whether that task be ordering the fields, or felling a tree, or mining, or questioning the laws of Nature, or determining the place of history in the force of destiny.

Knowledge means being in the place where we are put.

It is not so important for knowledge, as some people we know believe, whether or not it is something that originally grew in us, but it is important that we hold fast by our actions and our behavior to what we know. We no longer make a distinction between "educated" and "uneducated." And that is not because they are the same thing; we simply no longer place any value at all in this distinction. We do distinguish, however, between knowledge and the appearance of knowledge. The farmer, the craftsman and the scholar all have true knowledge, each after his own fashion, and in his field of work. On the other hand, the learned man may totally deceive himself by what is only the appearance of knowledge.

If you want to become rich in knowledge, it is not a question of getting yourself bits and pieces of some "general picture," as if you were being given charity. There must be awakened in you that knowledge by whose power you may become, each in his own place and specialty, clear and resolute German men.

Knowledge and its possession, as National Socialism understands these words, do not divide the classes, but rather bind and unite the people in the one great will of the State. Like the words "knowledge" and "scholarship," the words "worker" and "work" have taken on a new sound and a changed meaning. The "worker" is not, as Marxism would have him be, merely the opponent of exploitation. The working class is not the disinherited class marching to a general class war. "Work" is not simply the production of goods for others, nor is it merely the opportunity and means of getting a reward.

No. To us, "work" is the title of every regulated act and undertaking that is performed with responsibility toward the individual, the group and the State, and so becomes of service to the people. Work is found wherever, and only wherever, men's free power of decision sets itself to perform a task under the governance of a resolve. Work is therefore something spiritual in its own right, for it is founded upon freely acting knowledge of the circumstances, and regulated understanding of the work — that is to say, upon its own knowledge. The production of the miner is not fundamentally less spiritual than the action of the scholar.

"The workers" and "scholarly knowledge" form no contrast. Every worker is a learned man in his own way, and only as such can he work. The animal remains shut off from the privilege of work, which is denied to him. Every one who consciously decides and acts is a worker.

For this reason the resolve to throw up a living bridge cannot any longer remain an empty wish in you, any more than in us. The resolve to complete procurement of work by the procurement of knowledge must become in us inmost certainty, not flagging belief. For in what that resolve demands, we are but following the glorious will of our *Führer*. To become one of his loyal following means to desire wholeheartedly and undeviatingly that the German people may once more find its growing unity, its true worth and true power, and may procure thereby its endurance and greatness as a work State. *To the man of this unprecedented resolve, our Führer Adolf Hitler, let us give a threefold "Heil!"*

MARTIN HEIDEGGER

A DAY UNDER HEIDEGGER*

"Deploy when you march, close up when you fight!" This strategy has proven itself in many a war, but has undergone re-evaluation, like many things whose justification for existence lies only in the tarnished nobility to which they cling — and even this sometimes shows itself to be false. In recent times we have frequently been compelled to write in superlatives, when reporting the organization of the Freiburg National Socialist Party. The manner in which the Day of Honor of German Labor was celebrated in Freiburg was not only heartwarming and fully worthy of the significance of the day, it was also unique for Freiburg. There came to our reluctant minds the memory of May first of a year ago, of two, or five years ago, of the years before the First World War that was forced upon us — that war of the cannons against German competition in the world

* *Freiburger Zeitung,* May 2, 1933, page 2ff.

market, against German flesh, against German efficiency in every area of life without exception. At that time we saw — one might in today's mood of forgiveness and happiness prefer to forget about it, were it not that a too easy forgetfulness has been the source of many a day of mourning for Germany — we saw flags and posters bearing hate-filled words and symbols, not directed against the envy of foreign opponents, but against German brothers and sisters, against colleagues and comrades in the same plant, because they were more efficient and therefore more successful, because they did not labor with open hand, but were black-coat workers.

That the man in the overalls even pushed aside his work, while the other often struggled through the night as well as the day grappling with challenging problems, was neither appreciated nor valued. A physically and spiritually suicidal "equality" and leveling was king on that day. Whoever revolted against that king, and wished to improve himself for his own and his family's sake, was not merely ridiculed — he was thrown out of the company of those who "worked to rule." But now there is an end to this! Performance counts, and unity with the working community which recognizes no privilege but that of the coordination of all capable men of good will, at the command of its Fatherland, whose well-being and prosperity are far more closely bound up with that of the individual than is often recognized. "All are welcome, brothers and sisters of brain and brawn, so long as they think German, speak German and work German!"

Thus resounded the voice of Mayor Dr. Kerber over the (for Freiburg) unprecedented crowd in the Münsterplatz. And toward him were stretched in reply thousands and thousands of hands in the sacred oath of unbreakable loyalty and cooperation, heedless of the cost, in the work of Adolf Hitler.

——— ———

. . . On the Münsterplatz, since early morning, marches had been resounding through loudspeakers supplied by the firm of Schilling. Police and the SA here, as along the route of the procession, cordoned off the traffic in model fashion. The first to arrive, around eight-thirty, were the veterans with their war-disabled members, whom the Freiburg Automobile Club graciously transported in their cars. Benches had been erected for the comfort of these men, in front of the Dom Hotel. The head of the procession arrived at the Münsterplatz at about nine-fifteen. It was a group of riders on splendid horses. Then followed in an uncountable throng all the unions, the private, municipal and State chapters of the National Socialist organizations, the faculty of Freiburg University, the deacons in full regalia *under the leadership of the Rector, Martin Heidegger,* the student body with its officers, the Christian trades-unions, and so on.

In front of the Dom Hotel the singers took their place: the choir of Standarte 113, the flag delegations of the SA and SS. The student choral association Wettina had placed their rooms at the disposal of the Party, and there the highest leaders of State and municipal authorities — the leaders of the SA and SS, the delegates of the Stahlhelm, of the army associations, and so forth — gathered. The great Münsterplatz could hardly contain the throng of participants in the celebration, and yet the police and the auxiliary organizations of the *National Socialist Party* found room for them all.

The celebrations opened on the Münsterplatz at eleven o'clock with the anthem "Germany, to Thee My Fatherland," sung by the united Freiburg choral associations. In the religious service, Father Mohr represented the Catholic confession, and Pastor Albert, provincial leader of the German Christians, represented the evangelical sects.

Father Mohr referred to *Jesus Christ,* who chose his apostles from among the working people, and who took his teachings from the life of the people. Jesus Christ, he said, wished to free agriculture and the crafts from the insults of the heathen, and he reaffirmed the basic rule of humanity, that Almighty God calls men to work. Man shall labor with his hands, and all spiritual capacity shall unfold to the glory of God. Thou, O God, hast given us *Adolf Hitler* as our Leader, that he may bring us freedom and our daily bread, and that he may lead us through labor to see and to fulfill Thy service. Lord, *rule over us through Adolf Hitler,* and bless him with Thy light and Thy strength.

Pastor Albert began, "Where the master has no part in building the house, they that build it labor in vain." We in this hour acknowledge the plans of the men who have become master builders. Our praise is due to the first master builder, Adolf Hitler. The work that lies before us is so great that we might tremble before it unless we knew that over all stands the Lord, who gives strength and comfort, to all who call on him. Lord, bless the work, bless the master builder, bless the workers, deliver us from all need and make us free and strong. The Third Reich has become a reality. Now we must work, and build from the very foundations a new house. We must free the Church from the liberalism that hitherto held it in thrall. Workers with your hands, your soul was destroyed by the slogan "Class Warfare." To you comes now the word, Soul of Germany, awake! And you, workers with the intellect! The century of Liberalism turned the intellect into a false idol. To you, too, I say, Soul of Germany, awake! Know that in this very day God still performs miracles, and that the German soul will once more become strong. Before us stands the cathedral, a miraculous bulwark of German culture. The minister that looks down upon us should be to us a symbol and a comparison. Just as all of us here, workers with the brain and workers with the hand, have cooperated, so shall Germany become a single German cathedral, and we shall be called to labor and to build alongside one another. In this cathedral of German labor the soul of Germany shall once more find its everlasting strength and power, and so build a single magnificent Germany."

ANNOUNCEMENT FROM THE UNIVERSITY*

Yesterday there took place the inauguration of the weekly sport afternoon in the university stadium, and led to a significant announcement. The groups of sports associations marched in close order to the stadium, which was crowded with other students and members of the faculty. After the groups had marched round the central field, there followed the broadcast of Hitler's great speech from the Reichstag. *While we were still under the influence of the overpowering impression of the powerful warning addressed by the German Chancellor to the world, the Rector, Professor Heidegger,* made a short speech in which he said, among other things:

"The other peoples may choose which way they will go, after these words of the Chancellor. We are decided and resolved to take the hard road, that by our responsibility to posterity we are compelled to take. We now know the implications of this decision. They are readi-

* *Breisgauer Zeitung,* May 18, 1933, page 3.

ness to face the worst, and comradeship to the very last. Now let us go to work, and every small and great task of this semester shall stand under the sign of this readiness and comradeship."

After Professor Heidegger the President of the Academic Commission for Physical Training, Mr. Uhlenlut, heartily welcomed participants in the sports courses. It was a joy, he said, to see this new generation rejoicing in sports, and so-minded today, when the great physical and moral training schools of the former glorious army were lacking, of their own free will to organize and subordinate themselves in the community, and to develop from sports attitudes that would make them strong and healthy. In this sense sport is today a duty of the citizen and a duty of the student.

BOOK BURNING IN FREIBURG*

The student body of the University of Freiburg announces that it is determined to carry the fight against Jewish-Marxist undermining of Germany to the bitter end, to the complete annihilation of the foe. The public burning of Jewish-Marxist writings on May 10, 1933, served as a symbol of this fight. Germans, rally to this fight! Make your participation public, too! From the publishers and bookstores send us all books and writings that deserve burning. Let each one bring what he finds, or tell us about it so that we may go get it. The fire of destruction is to us like a blazing up of the German spirit and German custom and practice.

* *Breisgauer Zeitung,* May 18, 1933, page 3.

ANALYSIS AND SYNTHESIS*

From the Freiburg Student Paper

Here and there voices were raised, even at college, calling for synthesis. The first great, and indeed perfectly grandiose, attempt at synthesis in all areas is National Socialism. It rejects overvaluation of the point of view, and enunciates as central to our spiritual life the emotional values of freedom, honor, law-abidingness, comradeship, obedience and responsibility. It took us students out of the lecture halls, put us in the thick of the day-to-day political fight, and set us to spread the gospel of intellect and manual strength as the foundations of the true community of the people. *It recognized as decisive for the fate of a nation the synthesis of blood and land, and on that account fought against the homeless and rootless Jews who are born protagonists of analysis.* The name itself demonstrates the greatest synthesis. Nationalism and Socialism are, separately, empty concepts. Only in their union do they make sense. So much has been written in recent years on this subject that any recapitulation would be superfluous. The

* *Freiburger Studentenzeitung*, May 16, 1933, page 2.

gigantic spiritual revolution that National Socialism has set in motion cannot be without influence on the world of learning. The professors began to see that they exist for other ends than to dole out their knowledge at 2½ or 4½ marks per week-hour. *This development was spotlighted when our honored Rector, the philosopher Professor Heidegger, by his entry into the National Socialist German Workers' Party embraced the spiritual world of National Socialism.* Even though, according to the Professor, one cannot always clearly distinguish between appearance and reality, at any rate the future and our work will gradually turn appearance into reality.

Our position is clear: We fight now as always against the cold arrogance of the intellectual man, who thinks he can trample on our enthusiasm and warmth of feelings with flippancy and with pitying smiles. We scorn maturity of this kind that is seen in men without heart or feeling, and yet is nothing more than the destruction of all ideals, of everything that is beautiful and noble and that makes this life worth living. We reject every compromise with it, and will not turn from the fight on account of difficulties. We refuse to be turned into stereotypes by the colleges under the pretext of specialization; we will not leave the colleges after enjoying to the full the deceitful phrases of academic freedom such as *the* doctor, *the* lawyer, *the* pastor. We will leave, rather, as *a* doctor, *a* lawyer, *a* pastor. We will have none of these imperceptible, and therefore dangerous, suppressions of personal needs, but will cultivate individuality, naturally within the framework of the unifying idea. This has nothing in common with liberalism, but is an expression of the Leader principle!

If our professors heed these demands and add to them their own, German intelligence under the Third Reich will be *able to fulfill completely all the tasks imposed upon it by the Führer.*

TEACHING LICENSES OF JEWISH LECTURERS AT FREIBURG UNIVERSITY REVOKED*

By decree of the provincial governor (Robert Wagner) the teaching licenses of the following Jewish professors of Freiburg University were revoked in accordance with the law concerning the revocation of professional licenses: [NAMES].

The teaching licenses of Jewish professors in Heidelberg University and the Karlsruhe Technical College were also revoked.

* *Der Alemanne,* October 1, 1933, page 11.

FIRST DUELING CONTEST OF THE FREIBURG FENCING ASSOCIATION*

Say what you like about the fighting student, you'll never be able to say that the student fencing association is inclined to imperil German prestige abroad in the way that not long ago the Baden state government did when they passed a shameful prohibition against students exercising themselves in this knightly, character-forming and bodily-improving sport! On Saturday night the first dueling contest of the Freiburg fencing association took place in the Löwenkeller. The hall was decorated with flags and made a colorful spectacle. In honor of the *Führer* the *Horst Wessell Lied* was sung. The associations, carrying banners, ranged themselves on the fencing floor. Among the numerous guests present were many university professors, *including the Rector of the University, Professor Heidegger*. The state and municipal authorities came, together with representatives of the police. Five matches were fought in the middle of the hall.

* *Der Alemanne,* May 5, 1933, page 9.

THE GERMAN STUDENT IN THE NEW STATE*

In the municipal festival hall the academic Education Week opened on Monday. After the officers of the student body had marched in with their banners, the leader of the student body, Mr. Kunzel, greeted the assembly and especially the Rector, *Professor Heidegger,* together with the other professors present. He then spoke of the significance of the meeting, and stressed that *Adolf Hitler* had once said that without the German students he could not win his battle.

* *Freiburger Zeitung,* July 25, 1933, evening edition, page 6.

PROFESSOR HEIDEGGER IS A MEMBER OF THE NSDAP*

The Rector of Freiburg University, Professor Martin Heidegger, has made his official entry into the National Socialist Party. Prof. H. was born in Messkirch in 1889.

* *Breisgauer Zeitung*, May 4, 1933, page 3.

BEGINNING OF TERM AT FREIBURG UNIVERSITY*

The Rector of the University, Professor Heidegger, has recommenced his lectures. Last semester Professor Heidegger did not lecture. His lectures on the Foundations of Philosophy are sure to be well attended.

* *Der Alemanne,* May 5, 1933, page 9.

www.ingramcontent.com/pod-product-compliance
Lightning Source LLC
La Vergne TN
LVHW050945080826
845145LV00004B/1417

* 9 7 8 0 8 0 6 5 3 0 7 9 6 *